QUILLING WILL

ALICE-CATHERINE JENNINGS

ASSURE PRESS

Copyright © 2021 by Alice-Catherine Jennings

All Rights Reserved. No part of this book may be performed, recorded, used or reproduced in any manner whatsoever without the written consent of the author and the permission of the publisher except in the case of brief quotations embodied in critical articles and review.

An imprint of Assure Press Publishing & Consulting, LLC

www.assurepress.org

ASSURE PRESS

Publisher's Note: Assure Press books may be purchased for educational, business, or sales promotional use. For information please visit the website.

Quilling Will/Alice-Catherine Jennings — 1st ed.

ISBN-13: 978-1-954573-22-2
eISBN-13: 978-1-954573-23-9
Library of Congress Control Number: 2021930011

CONTENTS

How like a winter hath my absence been ...	1
Blood-red berries blush the wild bud haunts...	2
Mine eyes hath played the painter...	3
After "Desert Road" by Ellen McCarthy	4
Scraped Again	5
At Ristorante Ottava Nota in Palermo	6
Bengali Sweet House	7
Raj Mandir Cinema	8
Coyote Run	9
O Pōhutukawa	10
O Phainopepla	11
Watching a Clown Frogfish Feed	13
The Secret Is Laid Bare	14
Certificate of Survival	15
Exhausted Soil	16
Beware The Ides of March	17
Disobedience	18
Six Degrees of Detachment	19
White Ashes	20
Martha	21
Det är ingen ko på isen	22
I Send You A Ghost	23
Acknowledgments	25
About the Author	27

QUILLING WILL

How like a winter hath my absence been...

Water witching my way to the river I unclasp the iron
brackets of the clapboard gate—
the smell of brown green. The estuary renews
its force while the lichen pimples
the slabs of stone at the water's edge.
Crescano crescano crescano
églantier, ephedra & saule blanc.
I whisper wishes to make the world
sweeter before it snaps apart.
The better angel is a man right fair.
Though the wood of the willow is tough
it easily decays. Covered with goat droppings
I discover an unfound book *Look Homeward, Angel*.
I'm lost yet not alone.

How like a winter hath my absence been and *the better angel is a man right fair* are lines from Sonnets 97 and 144 by William Shakespeare.

Blood-red berries blush the wild bud haunts...

while the day lilies decompose
peptic citron in color pitiable
aside rustic herbage, spear shafts
sturdy of the chokeberries. The juice

of the *aronia* drips tints her fingers
as she harvests summer's bursting
fruit by stony steeps and ancient walls.
She stops to taste. *No bitterness that she*

will bitter think. Childless, running sore,
her womb atremble. Balance the intake
and the outtake she knows: the douches
in the womb, the waters with brewes

wort and iron, the sulfur and mallow—
double penance to correct correction.

Blood-red berries blush the wild bud haunts is a line from *The Georgics* by Virgil, as translated by Kimberly Johnson

No bitterness that I will bitter think is and *Nor double penance, to correct corrections* are lines from Sonnet 111 by William Shakespeare.

Mine eyes hath played the painter...

I drop the sable brush in water
and fill with paint.
Wet on wet I whisk whorls
of yellow clusters to form
a *limonier* or *cognassier*
perhaps...
I sgrafitto the unbranched stem
of the *bouillon blanc*

then light the sky with circles of clouds
until dusk has fallen. I tidy up and call
you in. I fool no one not even you.
I crinkle the cold-press paper
and toss it
into the tangled mess on the floor.

Mine eyes hath played the painter is a line from Sonnet 24 by William Shakespeare.

After "Desert Road" by Ellen McCarthy

I ghost quit my job, up and left
the asparagus plants— *Spargelzeit* be
damned! I escaped the white gold
in a blur of maps.
A liquid pris'ner pent in walls of glass
no more! The white angora swished
her tail la-di-da so up I packed the cat
plus my bikini pink & poof! In dust
and pebbles I bolted off.
To the clear day with thy much clearer light
…in time…in time…
the red desert of the sagebrush steppe
shimmered thru cracked windows.
…*this thy golden time*…

A liquid pris'ner pent in walls of glass…; *to the clear day with thy much clearer light*…; and…*this thy golden time*…are phrases from Sonnets 5, 43, and 3 by William Shakespeare.

"Desert Road" is an image by Ellen McCarthy.

Scraped Again

Where in the chronicle of wasted time,
I recall in the gossamer of my mind, Alan—
settled on that balcony in Rome savoring
Sri Lankan tea. Yes, it is just as before—
Alan in his cambric shirt and brown loafers
tapping warn and thin, *Time's pencil, or my*
...pen... he repeats. His lust-limp gaze as he
decodes the lines behind the lines behind
the lines ...of the *Codex Nitriensis*,
the whimpers of the heroic hexameter
of young men's cries abaft the postulates
of Euclid and Luke's epiphany on life.
Oh Alan! You craved the passages of
ancient quills but not my modern lips.

Where in the chronicle of wasted time and *Time's pencil, or my pupil pen* are from Sonnets 16 and 106 by William Shakespeare.

At Ristorante Ottava Nota in Palermo
    —After "Delight in Disorder" by Robert Herrick

The scarlet pulp on my linen dress
kindles in cloth the three days
watching the paste dry
—wooden tables
scraped sleek and clean—
that crimson sauce poured
from a sizzling pot
with chunks of onion, garlic,
and leaves of bay, olive green.

O bewitching heat!
Enthralled by the Sicilian
wine—that lusty red, I neglected
to drape the *tovagliolo* on my lap:
my Milanese frock now destroyed.

Bengali Sweet House
    —After Bernadette Meyer

did our teeth feel the sweet
pain?circular chewy sugar
dumplinged did we not eat
it all? rasgullah doughy white
cardoman flavored milky
solids lipsticked, unstick
gulabjamun ash gourd petha
did the finch eat the parakeet,
or the clouds blow over sunless
rivers? unhip, unkale, delish
alebi, rasgullah, gulabjamun
marigolds glowed orange
hubs of sun on string strung
hubs of sugar pretzel curls

Raj Mandir Cinema
—After Bernadette Mayer

Dolly, a FIVE POINT
SOMEONE a looteri
dulhan, a high shine
thief ululating calls
loud whee-oh torry-
yu mellow & fluffy
she patterns thievery
like the colors of

                      the fern-leaf
                      plastered walls
                      pink blue blue pink
                      crash the boy's heart
                      then another crashed
                      heart "no need to repeat."

Dolly Ki Doli is a 2015 Indian comedy-drama film about a young woman who is a con artist.

Coyote Run

I hear their yodeling in the northward
winds at night. By day, I walk the pup.
We trespass their trodden route along
the *arroyo* amidst the junipers, the piñon trees.
The pup—she has no name— chases the lizards
with their scaly backs as I look down for traces

of paw prints as well as shriveled scat. We stop!
The pup's ears stand up. *Such eyes!*
We spot them. A pack, a parent group—
the alpha female the one in charge—there's
the scent of territoriality. Perplexed by fear,

upon my leg, the pup, she leans and whines.
"Come on, pup," I say, "less ahead more behind."

Such eyes! is from "Coyote Brood" by Lew R. Sarett.

O Pōhutukawa

Will you survive when I in the earth
am rotten? I write you from my walnut
escritoire—the swish of my pen quivers.

I perceive your hearts sprout where
needed, sucking up *kātao,* the water.
Crimson, apricot, yellow & pink—

your peppy variations dazzle in bloom.
I've seen your cut outs on greeting cards
at Christmas, an erasure of Maori blood.

The possums strip your shoots
and the fires abuse your roots.
Ah New Zealand…

I itch for your green-lipped mussels.
Please world! *Treasure thou some place.*

Will you survive when I in the earth am rotten and *Treasure thou some place* are from Sonnets 81 and 6 by William Shakespeare.

O Phainopepla

jet-black
plumage
curled
atop
your puffy
scalp.
Let no
unkind,
nor beseechers
kill
deserts
woodlands,
your
bucolic
sites…

which by
and by
night
doth
take
away
checkered
cliffs
& bracing
creeks

by oil &
gas
extractive
thieves.

Let no unkind, nor fair beseechers kill and *which by and by night doth take away* are from Sonnets 135 and 73 by William Shakespeare

Watching a Clown Frogfish Feed
 —After "Watching the Sea Go" by Dana Levin

Twelve inches of globular softness
twelve inches of warty green,
biofluorescent spots of gold-fish
gold on benthic coral reefs.

Its lure
moves slowly to the left
then right
mimicking a worm. A pellucid camouflage
his prey sees as craggy rock.

Sheltered by pore-bearing growth—twelve inches
of dermal spinules, engulfing
fish twice
his size with his Hapsburg jaw. What hoaxer
is this who gapes and sucks such saps?

The Secret Is Laid Bare
   —*After D.H. Lawrence*

You tell me I am wrong.
Would you like to lob
a stone perchance
         —or a sorb-apple, a black fig?
America has gone dry. The squash
blossoms hang heavy, unpicked.
What is it that makes
         all the grapes turn to raisins?

I am drunk
with anger and fight to stay
         awake. Look at them
standing there
in authority—pale-faced
with tilted crowns.

Source: Lawrence, D. H. *Birds, Beasts and Flowers*. Shearsman Books Ltd, 2011.

Certificate of Survival

Beweep my outcast state, I am alone
shabby in the doldrums.
To chew over my state is banal,
I know. My bad smell incites me
to squabble with the others
on the bleak streets.
Such poverty—if only we could hide it.
That's what they want.
I trouble deaf heav'n with my bootless cry.
In bits of mental clarity, I crave
suspiros de monja, crisp fritters
round with creamy insides —
the nun's sighs, vestiges of my
former life.

I am alone beweep my outcast state, and *And trouble deaf heav'n with my bootless cries* are lines from Sonnet 29 by William Shakespeare.

Exhausted Soil

Flattened out, zip lined to zero
I feel the flames spear out & rip
through the gambrel of Our Lady—
Notre Dame…"*La flèche! La flèche!*"
the spectators sob as the spire collapses.
How can I then return in happy plight

to Paris? That roof—lattice of wooden
beams cut from trees in pristine forests.
Trees so huge they exist no more. Now I—
must weep for the trees! *And night doth…*
make grief's length seem stronger. And yet,
in Iraq when St. Elijah, Dair Mar Elia,

was crushed by ISIL fever, clouds did
not blot the heavens of my thoughts.

How can I then return in happy plight and *And night doth nightly make grief's length seem stronger* are lines from Shakespeare's Sonnet 28.

Beware The Ides of March

the time when Mars calls in Alecto
with her snakes for hair to gad about:

in a mosque a 3-year old lies limp
scorched earth remodels the remains
of those they hold dear, rubbish wrecks
a whale, perforce a stroke strikes my friend
ecreta covers the captive in internment
and by their own hands two teens die.

All too ready to welcome *proud-pied
April, dressed in all his trim*, I am absent
from a blinding headache.
*The very birds are mute
or if they sing, 'tis with so dull a cheer.*

Beware the Ides of March is a line from *Julius Caesar* by Shakespeare.

Proud-pied April, dressed in all his trim and *the very birds are mute/or if they sing, 'tis with so dull a cheer* are from Sonnets 98 and 97 by William Shakespeare.

Disobedience

The yellow roses arrived... not sure why.
Clip the stems—
I will not permit them to wilt...
not certain why.
Remove the excess
leaves & split the roses
down the center with that blade.
Dry & press... NO! that won't do:
seeds
cotyledons
radicles
dissect the order!
Where the bee sucks, there suck I...
Where's the hammer? My Dignity?

Where the bee sucks, there suck I is a line from Shakespeare's "The Tempest."

Six Degrees of Detachment
   —After "Chronicle" by Ruth Bavetta

i stare at the colored-pencil painting crosshatched lines hooked
to a notion of the beach boys is it the shorts the keds the
summer sandals close up six individuals of unimportance i
can only think of people disconnected flashbacks of pool
parties amidst the air of light all those people mingling how i
felt so hard and alone i scanned a new life story one about
jackie kennedy onassis did she really take pep pills and
downers to find camelot do we all dope up in some way
or another
to live in a castle with a moat was a half-hearted
fancy but that was before i knew about drawbacks think
the tudors six wives six characters in an artwork five men
one woman with an unused camera there's a policeman two
cones of warning yet no one seems concerned or attached
why not

"Chronicle" is a painting by Ruth Bavetta.

White Ashes

Cold is the absence of color. I read an article
not about global warming. We're on the verge
of a new ice age. No more almonds, avocados, apricots
nor apples. All will be caked with ice and cracked
like exposed skin in the desert. The butter will be frozen.
In art class, I place tiny ice cubes on a stainless steel island.
I am searching for simulacra. In autumn, cotton is like puffs
of snow in the delta. If economists were Southerners,
today's headlines would read: "We're all in low cotton."
L'Anguille, La Grue, Lula and *Lacy*. Crossing
the Mississippi on Hallows Eve, I hear an eerie noise—
a strangled cry from a colony of egrets. My sister
calls from France. "It snowed last night," she
screams as the tumor breaches her brain.

Martha

Chanting in the choir, she hinted at serenity
not hard edge chaos nor
persistent terror & tattered jitters.
At times she played the flute
vibrating the air through a hole, a black hole
so dense it swallowed her up. *Tir'd with all these,*
for restful death I cry,...
I taste that adaption dark and constant
a black silk dress—unchic—
that envelopes you in a place of gripped
grief. No, you will not be a beggar for salvation—
simple truth miscall'd simplicity. You are called
to be a burden to a poplar. Unless...
Save that, to die, I leave my love alone.

Quotations are from Sonnet 66 by William Shakespeare.

Det är ingen ko på isen

Since Alice died, the melons
refuse to swell, the roosters no
longer squat, and the skin of the ostrich
crackles. The desert air is damp
with a cacophony of hoo-ha din.
At evening's edge we eyeball the red
dwarf-dropping sun while we crimp our lips
along frost-ringed glasses and murmur
to ourselves. There's no cow on the ice
so no need to worry. It's all folly, age
and cold decay. The children of
the children of the children
will sprint amongst the yellow rabbit
brush and brood of her no more.

Det är ingen ko på isen is an idiom. The literal translation is "There's no cow on the ice." What it means is "There's no need to worry."

Folly, age and cold decay is from Sonnet 11 by William Shakespeare.

I Send You A Ghost

Freki & Geri, the two
wolves, sit by the fire

as Othin dictates
his dinner of cold tubers,

herring & chokeberry
wine. His house is wide-

shining, free from
untensils unclean.

Freki is greedy.
When will the tooth

gift arrive?
The fire is hot.

Linda, the poetess,
knocks at my door.

I send you a ghost is a line from "drop of blood" by Linda
Vilhjálmsdóttir.

ACKNOWLEDGMENTS

Grateful acknowledgment is made to the editors of the following publications in which these poems first appeared, sometimes in a slightly different form:

Pinnacle, a poetry anthology: "Mine eyes hath played the painter ..."
Zoomoozophone Review, Issue 6: "Bengali Sweet House" and "Raj Mandir Cinema"
Along the Shore, Poems of the Sea published by Lost Tower Publications: "Watching a Clown Frogfish Feed"
For a Better World 2019, Poems and Drawings on Peace and Justice: "The Secret is Laid Bare"
Phemme, Issue 2: "White Ashes"
Spit Poet Zine, published by Spit Poet Publishing: "Det är ingen ko på isen"
the quint, an interdisciplinary quarterly from the north, published by University College of the North in The Pas, Manitoba, Canada: "I Send You a Ghost"
Academy of the Heart and Mind: "How like a winter hath my absence been," "blood-red berries blush the wild bud haunts," Martha," and "After 'Desert Road' by Ellen McCarthy,"

Foreign Literary: "At Ristorante Ottava Nota, Palermo" and "Exhausted Soil."

Thanks to William Lee for surprising me one day with *Shakespeare's Sonnets, Edited with Analytic Commentary by Stephen Booth*, Yale University Press, 1977.

ABOUT THE AUTHOR

Alice-Catherine Jennings is the author of *Katherine of Aragon: A Collection of Poems* (Finishing Line Press, 2016) and *Notations: The Imagined Diary of Julian of Norwich* (Red Bird Chapbooks, 2017). Her poetry and translations have appeared in various publications worldwide. She lives in Santa Fe, New Mexico.

https://alicecatherinej.com

facebook.com/alice.jennings
twitter.com/AliceCatherine6
instagram.com/ecilaneaj